Managing Time on Purpose

Managing Time on Purpose

Dr. Deborah A. Johnson-Blake

"Managing Time on Purpose" Copyright © 2015 by Dr. Deborah A. Johnson-Blake

First Asta Publications, LLC paperback edition

All rights reserved. No part of this publication may be reproduced, stored in a retrieval system, or transmitted in any form or by any means without the prior permission of the publisher, except for brief quotations in reviews or articles.

Special Note: This book is based on a research study conducted by the author. All sources can be reviewed on the references page.

ISBN: 978-1-934947-94-4

Cover Designed by: Megan Pereen

Printed in the United States of America

Dedication

This book is dedicated to all leaders who want to manage time purposely to impact organizational success.

Contents

Introduction..ix

Chapter 1..1

Chapter 2..3

Chapter 3..10

Chapter 4..13

Chapter 5..19

Chapter 6..21

Chapter 7..25

Conclusion...28

Recommendations..31

References..33

Appendix A..37

Introduction

"Time is life. It is irreversible and irreplaceable. To waste your time is to waste your life, but to master your time is to master your life and make the most of it." - Alan Lakein

The management of time can be a struggle for you, as well as your staff, "Managing Time on Purpose" is a practical guide based on theory and best practices that can be used to effectively, efficiently, and purposefully manage your time and the time of your staff. As business leaders, it is important to recognize the importance of time management and the impact it has on your entire organization. In earlier times, people used the stars and planets' movement, the sun's shadow, and the moon's setting and rising as a way to measure time. Currently, calendars, clocks, and other technology serve as a scientific way to measure time. These measurements have helped people to become more effective and time conscious.

Effective managers and leaders recognize the correlation between time management and the impact it has on productivity in the workplace. In order for businesses to increase productivity, leaders [must] standardize their best practices, invest in essential people, develop processes, manage costs, and measure progress. Conquering and achieving these tasks require leaders to implement effective time management strategies. Good time management skills are vital for leaders like yourself, because the financial impact of mismanaged time could be detrimental to your organization's success. The maxim "time is money" represents savings for your company if employees are working productively. Before you can actively implement effective time management practices in your own organization, it is important that you understand the value of time, be able to identify, implement practical time management practices, and amend strategies that will benefit the entire organization. When awareness about the value of time management is increased, you are able to identify and implement practical time management initiatives, and be able to amend time management strategies on an ongoing basis. One of the major obstacles faced by managers is the recognition that there is a time management issue. The goal of "Managing Time on Purpose" is to serve as a resource and provide techniques that will help you as a business leader manage time efficiently, effectively, and purposefully.

CHAPTER 1

The Transformational Leader

"Don't encourage overtime. Tell your people that the best way to impress you is to do a great job in the time allotted for it and then go home and relax." – The Mafia Manager

Leadership is defined as the ability to persuade, inspire, and employ others to accept a shared vision. Transformational leaders provide visions for the future, encourage work groups, challenge followers' thinking, set high expectations, support the needs of subordinates, and act as role models. There are several different theories and styles as it pertains to leadership; however, for the purposes of this book, transformational leadership will be discussed. Spearheading time management initiatives involves a commitment to advocate change through productive leadership behavior and forms of inquiry. With dedicated leaders and employees, organizations have an opportunity for success as well as a chance to embrace innovation and performance excellence.

To follow the transformational leadership approach, your focus should be to guide daily beliefs that allow followers to accomplish your organization's vision and mission. This will shape the business culture. As an organization transforms, so does its culture. By building trust and accountability, you can motivate followers to embrace new initiatives, strategies, and systems to achieve organizational goals and objectives.

Discovering perceptions of time use and recognizing the impact on decision-making capabilities and processes is vital to managing time. Introducing productive change processes, such as fostering better time management skills, is as important as realizing the unconstructive impact nonproductive methods could have on change management and leadership effectiveness.

CHAPTER 2

Time Wasters

"Time is the scarcest resource and unless it is managed, nothing else can be managed." –Peter Drucker

Drucker's philosophy dictated that executives in top positions waste time continually on tasks that have little bearing on organizational success. The first step toward effectiveness is recording time use. A time log is valuable if you keep one on a monthly or weekly basis throughout the year so that better time management efforts can take precedence.

Managing time entails eliminating time wasters and unproductive tasks. Drucker (1967) suggested that executives should ask a series of problem-solving questions, including, "What would happen if this were not done at all?" (p. 36) "Which of the activities on my time log could be done by somebody else just as well, if not better?" (p. 37), and "What do I do that wastes your time without contributing to your effectiveness?" (p. 38) By asking these questions, you begin the process of recognizing time-consuming and unproductive activities and eliminating time wasters not only for yourself, but also for others (Drucker, 1967).

Once you record, analyze, and manage time, the final step is to determine the allotted time available to implement large tasks. Consolidating available time can begin with working from home one day a week (if permitted) or scheduling certain weekdays to work on major tasks or issues. The technique used to consolidate discretionary time is not as important as controlling the time. Since time is the scarcest resource, Drucker (1967) noted that everyone could track the sanction "know thy time", (p. 51) which is the catalyst toward time management effectiveness.

What are the main causes of lost or misused time in business? They are the result of poor crisis management: overstaffing, mal-organization, and information malfunction. Poor management on reoccurring crises is a "symptom of slovenliness and laziness" (Drucker, 2004, p. 42). In addition, a large workforce is ineffective, since people are often interacting with one another and not working. Whether done consciously or not, many time wasters disrupt work efforts, whether internal or external to the organization.

Common time wasters include poorly planned activities, miscommunication, poor information dissemination, and poor management. To combat this issue, Drucker reported that organizations are more likely to be effective when a streamlined workforce is in place with the skills and knowledge required to manage the business daily.

Time-wasting mal-organization is a symptom of unnecessary meetings. If you are spending more than 25% of your time in meetings you are wasting time (Drucker, 1967). Scheduling too many meetings indicates poor job composition, communication issues, and diffused responsibility among staff. The best solution is to not include top administrators in every meeting, but keep them abreast of the strategic decisions that require their attention.

A malfunction in information is the last time-waster (Drucker, 1967). The way disseminated information flows through organizational lines often prevents a person from receiving information. Time-wasting issues are simple to correct, but when issues do take longer to correct they expend time.

Controlling time wasters is essential to time management leadership and organizational success. Many of the challenges encountered in daily work lives cause people to waste time and energy on unnecessary tasks (Stack, 2000). Effective leaders ensure priorities are clear, successfully communicate organizational objectives, and train employees to be efficient time managers so company goals are met. Priorities for employees can sometimes become unclear and inconsistent, which poses a challenge for managing time (Weatherly, 2004). The best leaders create competence in others and an ability to manage time wisely in accordance with established goals (Weatherly, p. 35).

Draper (2006) discussed such time wasters as unplanned interruptions, inefficient meetings, clutter and disorganized data, procrastination and indecision, and lack of priorities. To improve time management, Draper suggested the use of technology, which includes smartphones, e-mail, and electronic applications (apps). To be effective time managers, individuals with busy workloads must exercise, eat regularly, drink plenty of water, utilize the right brain, rest, maintain associations with friends and family, and participate in hobbies and other non-work related activities.

Work–life balance is essential to success. Jenson (1998) posited that you can gain a balanced life by becoming "open, relaxed and confident" (p. 48), which leads to more creativity and attentiveness. Exemplifying a balanced life could impact how you manage your organization and time.

Many employees struggle with time management problems on a daily basis. In a 2005 survey conducted by Basex, Incorporated (as cited in Needleman, 2007), researchers found that distractions for the average full-time employee result in losing two hours of each workday. Another report indicated that employees waste 60 minutes per day ("Key Organizations Systems," 2007) in the office because of ineffective use of time.

Time management affects work efficiency. Interruptions play a major role in managing time and are one of the key issues of time management. Because daily interruptions are not avoidable, disturbances that affect the use of time need managing. Time is irreplaceable and requires effective time management skills to yield success (Pearce, 2007). The better employees can manage time, the more likely it is that they can resolve issues and complete projects on time.

Time management is an issue many leaders face (Berman, 2007) when attempting to multitask and prioritize, but challenges persist (Wagner, 2007). When leaders use time inefficiently, costly issues arise (Green & Skinner, 2005), which could impact organizational success and effectiveness. It is time to gain control of these problems in your workplace and life.

5 Ways to Eliminate Time Wasting Activities

"Assess time as if it were your nemesis by conquering and strategizing victoriously" – *Dr. Deborah Johnson-Blake*

Wasting time can be avoided with conscious efforts and techniques. By implementing five (5) easy strategies, leaders will increase overall effectiveness. These strategies include tackling easiest tasks first, breaking down complex tasks, creating to-do lists, using calendars, and eliminating distractions.

1. **Tackle the Easiest Tasks First.**

Compiling a list of easier tasks first, provides you more time to pay more attention to larger and more complex tasks. Each day my to-do list increases; however, to reduce tasks and stress, my strategy is to assess the list by ease, completion times and due dates. For instance, if my Monday to-do list consists of a proposal to draft, a report to complete, telephone calls and emails to return, website updates, staff assessments, and on-going program development, then I have a decision to make. Of course, my decision should factor in interruptions, unplanned meetings, instant messaging, and other time wasters to be most effective. In my opinion, replying to emails is easy because there does not have to be immediate two-way communication. Therefore, my task list would be in this order: return emails, website updates, report, proposal, staff assessments, telephone calls (late in the afternoon) and program development. This way, I can accomplish the easier and less timely tasks first and focus on the ones that require more time and effort.

2. Break Down Complex Tasks into Smaller Chunks.

Breaking down more complex tasks into smaller chunks allows you to accomplish the tasks in a more digestible manner. For instance, my tasks of on-going program development requires several steps to complete and is very time consuming. For this and similar tasks, I develop an outline of what is to be accomplished and the completion deadlines. For a lesser complex task in the program development matrix of never-ending to-dos, I allot less than one day to complete. For the more complex tasks of program development, time frames range from 3-5 days, 2-4 weeks, 2-3 months, or longer. Remember, it is important to factor in the lag time of receiving requested information from your colleagues and external resources.

3. Create Your To-Do List at the End of Your Work Day for the Next Business Day.

Before you complete your final task of the day, the last task you should be doing is to create a list of things you need to do for the next business day. This way, when you arrive at work, you are ready to go! This is usually not a time consuming because you can simply assess your list of tasks you did not accomplish today and prioritize them for tomorrow. By doing this, you are setting yourself up for success for the next business day, which reduces and gives you something to strive for during your work days.

4. Use a Calendar to Keep Track of Everything.

I use my iPhone calendar to manage my life every day. I put everything on my calendar! If there is someone I know I should call in two months, I will create an Microsoft Office

Outlook task to follow-up on the date intended. If I have a speaking engagement or need to follow-up with a potential, I will place it on my electronic calendar. This makes life much easier and you reduce the chances of forgetfulness, making you more efficient. Another trick I do is to schedule two reminders for every event; one that occurs a day before and the other that happens 1-2 hours before the event. This way, I never miss important meetings or tasks that need to be completed.

5. Ignore Distractions as Best as You Can.

There are so many things that can get you off-track including phone calls, instant messages, interruptions by co-workers, or Facebook messages. You need to ignore as many distractions as possible so you can stay focused on completing your to-do list. A simple way to do this is to block off a half hour each day to just focus on the distractions and nothing else. The more distractions you encounter, the harder it will be to achieve your goals and reduce stress throughout the day.

CHAPTER 3

Importance of Time Management

"One always has time enough, if one will apply it well."
- Johann Wolfgang von Goethe

The paradigm shift from the adage of doing more with less is of days past, and today's new focus is on quality rather than quantity. The better you manage time, the more likely opportunities exist to resolve issues and complete projects in a timely manner. Ultimately, organizations whose leaders implement their best practices, such as time management, will become more successful than organizations that do not use them.

Time management scholar Lakein, the "inventor of time management" (as cited in Porter, 1999, p. 41) provided valuable insight on controlling time. Lakein argued that there exists "no such thing as lack of time" (p. 12), but only the need for a more effective use of time. According to Lakein, the objective of time management is to set priorities and goals, and individuals work most effectively toward goals in increments of 15, 30, and 60 minutes.

Time is one commodity that all people wish they had more of because limited time is available in each workday. Each person's perception of time is different and all offer various time strides in time management. Lee and Lee (1991) discussed four types of time strides: the overachiever, the self-disciplined, the "chase-your-own-tail", and the careless (p. 6).

Four types of Time Strides

The overachiever. The overachiever denotes the Type-A personality and overextends him or herself to the point of burnout. It is critical for the overachiever to take breaks (Lee & Lee, 1991). Stop and take a dip in the ocean. If you find yourself burned out from time-to-time, post a snap shot of your favorite vacation spot in the office and in your car. Take 1-2 minute mini breaks throughout the day viewing the photo and visualizing yourself there or planning your vacation. Remember, it is okay to say no sometimes! Once your "vacation break" is over, reassess your to-do list and calendar and only commit to the tasks that are priority and realistic within your work day/week. Also, delegation should be an important component of your work day. You can't do it all alone!

The self-disciplined. The self-disciplined individual is well-balanced and recognizes the importance of possessing an even-keel life. You are at the top of the game recognizing that a balanced professional and personal life is key to your sanity. However, sometimes your button needs to be loosened because there is seldom 50/50 balance in a leader's life! As a result, allow for flexibility and the opportunity to work in a 60/40 environment periodically. Eventually, a more even-keel life balance will result from time to time (Lee & Lee, 1991).

The "chase-your-own-tail". The chase-your-own-tail personality accomplishes his or her objectives but is unsystematic and represents the Type-C personality. The catalyst to the downfall of the Type-C personality is blaming others for one's inability to be an effective time manager (Lee & Lee, 1991). I am sure you have encountered this person in your office.

The careless. Finally, the individual who does not care about time is unproductive. Unproductive individuals are not positive assets to the organization and should be coached to improve or the alternative (Lee & Lee, 1991). These are workers that will not serve the organization well. It is time to get off the bus as Jim Collins would insist.

Chapter 4

Principles of Time Management Strategies

Never let yesterday use up today. - Richard H. Nelson

Before you can improve time efficiency, you must understand the meaning of time. Hobbs (1997) defined time as "the occurrence of events one after another and define[d] management as the act of controlling (p. 8)." Kleinmann (2007) and Koch (1998) defined time management as "the self-controlled attempt to use time in a subjectively efficient way to achieve outcomes" (p. 201). Kleinmann and Koch indicated that one's choices determine time management. Time management is the ability to spend time on important achievable tasks.

The premise behind time management is to for people to do more with less time (Harung, 1998). The implementation of effective time management strategies can be problematic for many managers, because of the lack of support and the cooperation from those involved. Time management focuses on the timing of tasks and creating more products (Harung). Individuals who ineffectively manage time experience stress as projects go unfinished, a fact which results in low efficiency and ineffectiveness (Thairu, 1999). Ineffective time management results in lower task achievement and feelings of overburden (Thairu).

Stack (2000) described three key time management principles beneficial to leaders:

1. *Keep employees from burning out*

Employees become easily overwhelmed when charged with completing several important projects at once. An increased workload often results in a lower quality of work and diminished effectiveness. A good management technique to prevent burnout is to look for signs such as fatigue, working excessive long hours, and distractedness. Effective leaders listen to staff to discern workload levels, and help employees develop effective time management strategies (Stack, 2000).

2. *Model effective time management behavior*

Practicing good time management habits will encourage your employees to follow suit. Exerting proactive behavior and limiting crisis management modes helps leaders reduce unproductive tasks, delegate assignments, and simplify work life (Stack, 2000). When employees work in crisis regularly, begin effective time managers is challenging.

3. *Eliminate activities that waste time*

Figure out what matters most and empower yourself and others to develop the abilities to accomplish pre-determined objectives. Remove obstacles and eliminate opportunities to procrastinate.

Overall, time management is the ability to spend time on important achievable tasks. As the work environment transforms, many of your employees will be faced with new work challenges and will attempt to juggle numerous tasks with limited amount of time, which often leads to procrastination. There are several strategies you can use to help manage your time and the time of your employees, which include: scheduling time better, prioritizing, using technology, organizing workspace, managing lists, completing projects, and declining tasks.

O'Brien (2003) recommended tactics that can help with accomplishing these strategies include:

1. Maintaining a time log, you can assess how time is spent.
2. Eliminate those time wasters that do not impact the mission of the organization.
3. Work smarter by accomplishing task during the most productive times of your day.
4. Be diligent in accomplishing important tasks and reduce interruptions.
5. Use the latest technology to improve your productivity. Technology includes smartphones, applications (apps), software, and similar devices. Suggested time management and organizational apps include MyLifeOrganized, DocuSign, Evernote, Toggl, JotNot, Microsoft Outlook, Basecamp, Bugme, Toodled, and Checklist Wrangler. You select the applications that work best for you and your commitments.
6. Organize your workspace by ensuring everything has its place and by keeping the most used items accessible.

Another effective time management strategy is the creation and management of "to-do lists. You can organize your to-do lists into five lists in sequential order: projects, next actions, waiting for, calendar, and someday/maybe (Allen, as cited in O'Brien, p. 39).

- Projects Lists focus on vision.
- Next actions are subsequent steps enumerated on the priority list.
- Waiting-for Lists are dependent on others for completion.
- Calendar Lists are time-based appointments and meetings.
- Someday/Maybe Lists contain items not ready for the projects list.

Other strategies include understanding what is important, how to set realistic deadlines for completion, and the ability to say no to projects.

When you practice good time management habits, employees will experience the trickle-down effect of your behavior. In addition, exerting proactive behavior and limiting crisis management modes helps you reduce unproductive tasks, delegate assignments, and simplify work life (Koch, 2003).

An important principle to consider as a business leader is the 80/20 principle, which suggests that 80% of job achievement (output) results from 20% of work effort (input) (Koch, 1998). This theory originated from the Pareto law (as cited in Koch, 1998), which was a study of wealth distribution conducted in England in the 1800s. The Pareto theory indicated that "causes, results, outputs, inputs, and efforts and rewards" (p. 4) are disproportionate, including wealth allocation; hence, the birth of the 80/20 principle. In a business context, 80% of profits come from 20% of customers (Koch, 2003).

Individuals can do more with less, and adopting the 80/20 principle is the method to achieve success. Koch (2003) provided a unique approach to discussing time and its influence on the business world by combining Einstein's general theory of relativity and Pareto's law. Koch paraphrased Einstein's relativity theory, indicating that four dimensions of space exist instead of three. The fourth entity is time, and the business world has not accepted that time is relative.

According to Koch (2003), "time is an integral part of what we do and who we are. Time is a dimension where, like space, we can express ourselves and create a value for others, and therefore ourselves (p. 84)." With the combination of both Einstein's and Pareto's premises, Koch noted that if "80 percent of the wealth (or anything else desirable) is created in less than 20 percent of time available, then there is no shortage of time" (p. 84). Hence, a lack of time does not exist and individuals can do much more with less time. Under the doctrine of the 80/20 principle, you can accomplish 60% more by working a two-day workweek.

Cutting time involves devising an action plan with time measurements visibly indicated so you can analyze time use. The time between completing tasks oftentimes does not bring value to an organization. The Boston Consulting Group (as cited in Koch, 2003) indicated, "10% of the total time devoted to any work in an organization is truly value-added. The rest is wasted because of unnecessary steps or unbalanced operations" (p. 89). Planning before acting is crucial to the success of the 80/20 principle, which prompts individuals to exhibit their innermost business creativity. Similar to other scholars in the time management arena, Koch noted that identifying a person's most valuable activities and linking those high-value activities to a new idea generally results in success. If you understand the importance of time, you can effectively manage it and achieve success.

Time exists so tasks can happen, and to experience time as a valuable resource (Kearns & Gardiner, 2007) leaders need to know how to manage it resourcefully with the lowest costs. Time management, measured by numerous means, is a compilation of strategies to control time effectively. Quality time is the process of productively using time in a succinct manner to accomplish objectives. Future time is the basis for time horizon, and upper management typically supervises with a focus on long-term organizational objectives. Thinking time is the opportunity to be creative and solve issues and can be incorporated into the workday or workweek. Flextime allows employees to design their schedules based on individual time constraints and generally results in higher productivity with the correct implementation (Thairu, 1999).

Time management consists of three components: personal time management, organizational time management, and time management training for others within an organization (Thairu, 1999). Time management improvement depends on the analysis, design, and implementation of an effective action plan to promote increased productivity and efficiency. Categorizing organizational strengths and weaknesses as well as providing suggestions for improvement is crucial to determining time efficiency. An analysis provides insight into the issues of current organizational time management use, in addition to providing ways to improve time management effectiveness. To achieve optimum quality improvement and efficacy in time management, organizational cultures have to change (Thairu).

The last phase is implementing time management, which involves commitment to ensure compliance through several methods, such as work plans, planners, charts, and calendars (Thairu). Thairu (1999) suggested several techniques to gain the buy-in and empower employees. These techniques include encouraging an exchange of ideas and providing the benefits of adopting effective new styles of time management. You can work cooperatively with employees to monitor and evaluate effectiveness of new time management styles and empower staff to devise a time scale implementation plan that includes allocation of resources and responsibilities (Thairu).

Chapter 5

Good to Great

"Greatness is not a function of circumstance. Greatness, it turns out, is largely a matter of conscious choice and discipline." - Jim Collins

There are five hierarchical levels of executive leadership capabilities, with Level 1 as the lowest on the pyramid and Level 5 as the highest. Level 1 is not a demeaning role for leaders, because leaders at this level are very capable of leading. Each succeeding level includes the previous level (Collins, 2001).

According to Collins (2001), the goal is to strive to be a Level 5 leader, which is not indicative of every leader and organization. Level 1 leaders are highly capable individuals who exhibit good work habits and possess knowledge, skills, and abilities. As you move up the pyramid, you become more competent. Level 2 encompasses Level 1 as well as having the attributes of a contributing team member. Level 3 managers are proficient in organizing individuals toward organizational objectives and goals. Next, Level 4 leaders pursue high performance standards aligned with the organizational vision. The final objective is to become a Level 5 executive who "builds enduring greatness through a paradoxical blend of personal humility and professional will (p. 20)." The Level 5 leader is also known as the good to great leader.

Collins (2005) noted that the framework for the principles

of transitioning from good to great are the processes to build up and break through. Level 5 leadership is the catalyst to ignite building an organization from good to great. You must first determine whom you want on your team by replacing low performers and organizing the right people in the right areas of the organization. After the right people are in place, you must set an action plan to determine your vision. Third, you should acquire an ability to use the Stockdale paradox (p. 13). This involves the mindset that failing is not an option no matter the difficulties encountered, and facing reality is important to confronting the brutal facts. Fourth, embracing a culture of discipline is vital to being a great company. The culture of discipline includes disciplined people, disciplined thought, and disciplined action. By adopting a combination of the three disciplines and an entrepreneurial spirit, greatness is sure to ensue.

Technology usage is another stimulator for organizations to move from good to great. You must circumspectly choose technology. When coupled with forward thinking and pioneer-based transformation, your organization can become great. Remember that revolutionary changes are slow and continual.

Whereas Collins (2001) focused on ensuring that organizations transition from good to great, other scholars focused on individuals' perceptions of time and the impact this phenomena has on organizational culture and success. Let us take a look at how their thoughts can help you and your business.

Chapter 6

Time Perception and Plague of Time

"Time is a created thing. To say "I don't have time" is to say "I don't want to." – Lao Tzu

Brown and Herring (1998) stated that people's sense of time is either fast or slow. Time appears to pass quickly when events are good and fun, and slowly when they are bad or boring. In addition, cultural differences exist concerning the perception of time. An example of this is the use of the word tomorrow. Tomorrow has a connotation of "the next day" in England, but in Spain it means "sometime" (Brown & Herring). According to Brown and Herring, the "human mind does not treat time as an absolute, but as a highly variable phenomenon, dependent on a variety of internal and external factors" (p. 583).

Green (1975) and Gibson (1975) both believed that perception of time does not exist. Green (1975) reported, "We do not experience time, per se, but only what goes on in time, and the experience of time has both quality and quantity" (p. 2). Gibson (1975) agreed that "there is no such thing as the perception of time, but only the perception of events and locomotion" (p. 295). Identifying time perception promotes opportunities for you as leaders to understand the importance of time management. How you implement time management strategies to achieve optimum effort toward improvement is important as well.

Time management has plagued leaders and organizations since the early 1900s [as documented in scholarly journals], and the issue continues to stress some leaders. Robert Half Management Associates found that 46% of 1,400 chief financial officers indicated that time management was their largest challenge (Pomeroy, 2006). This figure represented a 10% increase from the previous 5 years. The organization attributed the rise to increased responsibilities and functions. How can you overcome these challenges?

Cox (2006) suggested tackling time issues first by renaming the dilemma and giving the problem rooms or compartments to handle tasks. Viewing each work shift as a container of time and prioritizing accordingly, helps you to manage time. The essence of Cox's strategy is to learn how to manage self and time, control which items go into each room, take ownership of self-behavior, and provide new options for managing time. The problem with managing self is to recognize one's response to others, not what others are doing. Determining the top priorities for the workweek and focusing on those main items provides a sense of better time management, especially if you schedule high-energy projects during peak hours of the day. Another strategy is to stay on track and focus on changeable and manageable tasks and projects rather than worrying about issues that one cannot control. Try tackling larger projects in smaller steps to prevent feeling overwhelmed. Managing self and time could cause resistance among your colleagues, but to avoid burnout, find reinforcement in those who support your new ways. (Cox, 2006)

Hart-Hester (2003) discussed six time management strategies in an article focusing on the secrets of effective leaders. Effective time management strategies included establishing goals, developing to-do lists, establishing efficient routines, delegating, setting timelines, and allowing down time.

Identifying your goals is important to determine task completion objectives daily, weekly, or yearly. In addition, setting timelines, being specific, and prioritizing achievable objectives will allow success. To-do lists are indispensable when determining daily tasks by priority of importance, but realize that many tasks on to-do lists are often not achievable and daily reassessment of your lists is necessary (Hart-Hester, 2003). A third strategy to save time is to create efficient, daily work routines that allow staff to analyze current efforts and task practices as well as eliminate inefficient methods of working. Another time-saving tactic is to delegate tasks to others in the office who can complete them. Last, scheduling down time is critical to becoming an effective time manager. Time away from office stress is important to becoming efficient and more in control of your time (Hart-Hester).

Motivation is the key to creating time power (Tracy, 2004). Having the desire is necessary to be a successful time manager. Ineffective decision-making is one of the prevalent culprits of robbing time. Doing more in less time is the prevailing philosophy regarding time management scholars; although the practice does not demonstrate effective time management and leads to increased stress. Making the best use of time is a challenge for all people, and identifying time wasters is fundamental to becoming a time efficient leader (Sawi, 2000).

Sawi (2000) also discussed six techniques to balance work and life. These are prioritizing, delegating, simplifying, setting time limits, procrastinating, and eliminating. Two effective time savers are procrastination and elimination. Procrastination involves the postponement of low priorities that eventually become unimportant to one person or important to another. Elimination is permanently deleting a task from your to-do list (Sawi).

It is also important to control your life events and determine your reaction levels to events that are uncontrollable. In providing a depiction of a control continuum, Smith (1994) indicated that some events are controllable and some are uncontrollable, and anything that lands in between you are able to partially control. After you discern that uncontrollable events require adaptation and less stress, you can have better control over not only your life but also your time.

Smith (1994) provided a different concept to prioritizing by coining the term laser thinking (p. 103), which is the ability to determine life's highest personal and professional priorities and which ones command the most value. Laser thinking begins in the planning stages, in which "time and energy is spent on daily activities through the lens of your governing values and goals" (p. 104). Instead of focusing on mundane tasks, concentrate on future goals and aspirations because prioritizing is the catalyst to effective time management.

Chapter 7

Organizational Success and Effectiveness

"There is nothing so useless as doing efficiently that which should not be done at all."– Peter F. Drucker

By analyzing time use, you can discover inefficiency and ensure your organization attains its mission and improves results. Stout (2001) suggested applying an evaluation technique termed Activity-Based Time Management (ABTM) to organizations to measure success. The goal of ABTM is to relay the amount of time your organization uses to accomplish desired results. Applying ABTM to organizations provides a snapshot of how time is allocated. You can evaluate the time spent on activities and implement useful tools to maximize organizational success, as well as provide a guideline on how staff members use time.

Kearns and Gardiner (2007) determined which time management behavior is the most effective in achieving success. Based on their experience, they chose to focus on the following behaviors:

1. Developing clear purposes in careers;
2. Planning and prioritizing;
3. Avoiding interruptions and distractions; and
4. Improving organization skills (p. 237).

Kearns and Gardiner (2007) found that participants perceived themselves to be more productive and effective when using the above time management behaviors. They found that respondents who had a clear purpose were most effective, and disorganized participants were the least effective. Kearns and Gardiner's findings showed that "some time management behaviors are able to predict perceived effectiveness and work-related morale and stress better than others (p. 246). To ensure effectiveness throughout organizations, Johnson-Blake (2010) proposed a Leadership Competency Model that could effect change and success organizational-wide.

Leadership Competency Model

Johnson-Blake's (2010) proposed Leadership Competency Model (See Appendix A) is a design that proposes effectiveness; however, it is important that the design:

1. Be appropriate to the culture;
2. Innovation is supported by stakeholders;
3. Is an understood system-wide process;
4. Processes are diversified; and
5. Resources are properly allocated.

By designing an ethical framework that focuses on organizational identity and responsibility, you can eliminate the guesswork about your role and obligations. Aligning practices with principles will help you become more committed to organizational success. By reducing cynicism, you present an opportunity to promote acceptance of ethical values. The process for resolving ethical conflicts involves your ability to solve problems as they develop. A significant gap exists between ethical values and behavior. However, effective leaders attempt to close the gap by continually applying the best strategies.

As you likely already realize, effective leadership is essential to success. Cashman's discussion on leadership composition revealed obvious characteristics of effective leadership, including:

1. Being a visionary;
2. Possessing integrity;
3. Being effective;
4. Having compassion; and
5. Having the courage to act sensibly under any conditions (p. 4).

Leaders who possess these characteristics and are team players tend to be more effective than others. Without a leader's vision and guidance, subordinates mishandle daily tasks and assignments. This ultimately yields a negative impact on an organization.

Conclusion

"There is a time in the life of every problem when it is big enough to see, yet small enough to solve." – Mike Leavitt

An effective leader ensures time management systems are in place to improve organizational success. Time management is essential to maintaining a balance between work and personal life for you as a leader as well as your staff members. Time management is essential to work productivity, and its effective use could reduce stress. Determining perceptions of time use and recognizing one's impact on decision-making capabilities and processes is crucial to managing time and executing strategies toward improving organizational success. Those who manage time effectively have more time.

Time is a scarce resource among many organizations (Berman, 2007; Thairu, 1999; Williams, 1996), and managing time is challenging and requires self-discipline if success is to be achieved. Leaders need to be prepared to use effective time management tools that promote organizational success. If you, as a leader, are committed to becoming more effective in achieving missions and attaining goals, you should recognize that managing time is critical to organizational success and the implementation of effective time management strategies is essential. Once leaders train, identify, and implement learned time management strategies and management skills, the organization can succeed even more.

Continuous improvement is crucial to achieving organizational goals. Transformational leadership is recognized as one of the leadership styles that creates a "culture high-performance working" (Daunton & Moss, 2006, p. 50) environment. Transformational leadership is the classic style that embraces innovation and change initiatives. By transforming leaders' perceptions of time to meet organizational objectives, opportunities exist for leaders to execute time management.

Recommendations

"Lack of direction, not lack of time, is the problem. We all have twenty-four hour days." – Zig Ziglar

The implementation of effective time management strategies impacts the entire organization. Working toward organizational success is a continual process and requires leaders of organizations to be the catalyst that sets the standards to achieve success. The following is recommended:

1. Make time management a high priority and communicate the importance of its effects to achieve organizational success for all stakeholders.
2. Solicit input from all stakeholders regarding effective time management strategies.
3. Adopt effective time management programs that benefit all stakeholders within your organization. Implementing an effective time management system could improve funding efforts and timely task completion.
4. Reinforce and support continual professional development that focuses on improving organizational change.

References

Brown, R. B., & Herring, R. (1998). The circles of time: An exploratory study in measuring temporal perceptions with organizations [Electronic version].*The Journal of Managerial Psychology,* 13, 580-602. Retrieved August 11, 2007, from the EBSCOhost database.

Cashman, K. (2003). *Awakening the leader within.* Hoboken, NJ: John Wiley and Sons.

Collins, J. C. (2001). *Good to great: why some companies make the leap...and other's do not.* New York, NY: Harper Collins.

Collins, J. C. (2005). *Good to great and the social sector.* New York, NY: Harper Collins.

Common Rule, 45 C.F.R. § 46.115 (2007). Retrieved January 4, 2009, from http://www.gpoaccess.gov/cfr/retrieve.html

Cox, S. (2006). Better time management: A matter of perspective [Electronic version].*Nursing,* 36(3), 43. Retrieved August 18, 2007, from the EB
SCOhost database.

Daunton, L., & Moss, G. R. (2006). Crack the leadership combination to secure high- performance working [Elec tronic version]. *People Management,* 12(17), 50. Retrieved October 21, 2008, from the EBSCOhost database.

Draper, L. (2006). Managing the workload [Electronic version]. *Foundation News & Commentary,* 47, 12-19. Retrieved July 23, 2007, from the EBSCOhost database.

Drucker, P. F. (1967). The effective executive. New York, NY: Harper & Row.

Drucker, P. F. (2004). *The daily Drucker.* New York, NY: HarperCollins.

Duncan, P. (2008). *The time management memory jogger: Create time for the life you want*. Salem, NH: GOAL/QPC.

Gibson, J. (1975). *The study of time II. Proceedings of the Second Conference of the International Society for the Study of Time*. In J. T. Fraser & N.

Hart-Hester, S. (2003). Time managers: secrets of effective leaders [Electronic version]. *Internet Journal of Emergency & Intensive Care Medicine, 7*(1). Retrieved February 20, 2007, from the EBSCOhost database.

Hobbs, C. H. (1987). T*ime power: The revolutionary time management system that can change your personal and professional life*. New York, NY: Harper & Row.

Jenson, D. (1998). In search of the balanced leader. *Nonprofit World, 16*(6), 48-50. Retrieved January 5, 2009, from the EBSCOhost database.

Johnson-Blake, D. A. (2010). Nonprofit administrators' perceptions of time use and effective time management strategies that impact organizational success (Doctoral dissertation). Retrieved from ProQuest Dissertations Publishing. (3405500)

Kearns, H., & Gardiner, M. (2007). Is time well spent? The relationship between time management behaviors, perceived effectiveness and work-related morale and distress in a university context [Electronic version]. *Higher Education Research & Development, 26*, 235-247. Retrieved January 11, 2009, from the EBSCOhost database.

Koch, R. (1998). *The 80/20 principle: The secret to success by achieving more with less*. New York, NY: Doubleday.

Lakein, A. (1973). *How to get control of your time and your life*. New York, NY: Penguin.

Lawrence. (Eds.), *Events are perceivable but time is not*. New York, NY: Springer-Verlag.

Lee, M. P., & Lee, R. S. (1991). *Coping through effective time management*. New York, NY: Rosen Publishing Group.

Needleman, S. E. (2007, January 9). How organization helps make most of a day [Electronic version]. *Wall Street Journal*. Retrieved September 3, 2007, from http://online.wsj.com

Pomeroy, A. (2006). Executive briefing: Time management challenges CFOs [Electronic version]. *HR Magazine, 51*. Retrieved August 1, 2008, from http://www.shrm.org/hrmagazine/articles/1206/1206execbrief.asp

Porter, M. V. (1999). Got a moment?[Electronic version] *Association Management, 51*(3), 41-43. Retrieved January 11, 2009, from the EBSCOhost database.

Sawi, B. (2000). *Coming up for air: How to build a balanced life in a workaholic world*. New York, NY: Hyperion.

Smith, H. (1994). The 10 natural laws of successful time and life management: *Proven strategies for increase productivity and inner peace*. New York, NY: Warner Books.

Stack, L. (2000). Looking at time through the lens of leadership [Electronic version]. *Employee Relations Today, 27*(3), 29-35. Retrieved August 25, 2007, from the EBSCOhost database.

Stout, W. D. (2001). A new way to evaluate your organization's performance: Measure your use of time [Electronic version]. *Nonprofit World, 19*(4), 29-31. Retrieved August 1, 2007, from the EBSCOhost database.

Thairu, W. (1999). Management of organizations in Africa: A handbook and reference. In J. Muruku Warguchu, M. Mwaura, & E. Tiagha (Eds.), *Time management in Africa* (pp. 281-293). Westport, CT: Quorum Books.

APPENDIX A:

NONPROFIT LEADERSHIP COMPETENCY MODEL

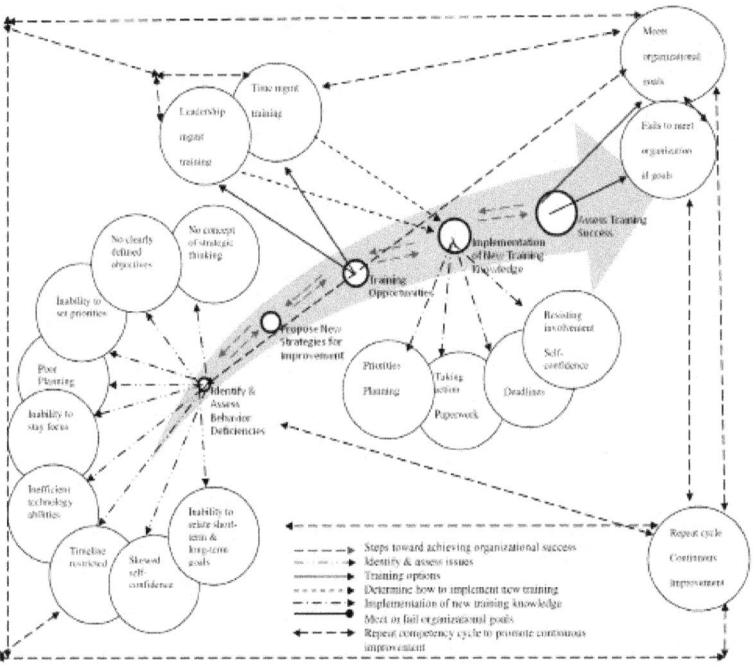

www.ingramcontent.com/pod-product-compliance
Lightning Source LLC
LaVergne TN
LVHW051210080426
835512LV00019B/3194